ISAAC ASIMOV'S NEW LIBRARY OF THE UNIVERSE

OUR PLANET EARTH

BY ISAAC ASIMOV
WITH REVISIONS AND UPDATING BY FRANCIS REDDY

Gareth Stevens Publishing
MILWAUKEE

For a free color catalog describing Gareth Stevens' list of high-quality books, call 1-800-542-2595 (USA) or 1-800-461-9120 (Canada). Gareth Stevens' Fax: (414) 225-0377.

Library of Congress Cataloging-in-Publication Data

Asimov, Isaac.
  Our planet Earth / by Isaac Asimov; with revisions and updating by
Francis Reddy.
      p. cm. — (Isaac Asimov's New library of the universe)
  Rev. ed. of: Earth: our home base. 1988.
  Includes bibliographical references and index.
  ISBN 0-8368-1194-1
  1. Earth—Juvenile literature. [1. Earth.] I. Reddy, Francis, 1959-.
II. Asimov, Isaac. Earth: our home base. III. Title. IV. Series: Asimov,
Isaac. New library of the universe.
QB634.4.A86   1995
550—dc20   94-32484

This edition first published in 1995 by
Gareth Stevens Publishing
1555 North RiverCenter Drive, Suite 201
Milwaukee, Wisconsin 53212, USA

Project editor: Barbara J. Behm
Design adaptation: Helene Feider
Editorial assistant: Diane Laska
Production director: Susan Ashley
Picture research: Kathy Keller
Artwork commissioning: Kathy Keller and Laurie Shock

Printed in the United States of America

1 2 3 4 5 6 7 8 9 99 98 97 96 95

To bring this classic of young people's information up to date, the editors at Gareth Stevens Publishing have selected two noted science authors, Greg Walz-Chojnacki and Francis Reddy. Walz-Chojnacki and Reddy coauthored the recent book *Celestial Delights: The Best Astronomical Events Through 2001.*

Walz-Chojnacki is also the author of the book *Comet: The Story Behind Halley's Comet* and various articles about the space program. He was an editor of *Odyssey*, an astronomy and space technology magazine for young people, for eleven years.

Reddy is the author of nine books, including *Halley's Comet, Children's Atlas of the Universe, Children's Atlas of Earth Through Time,* and *Children's Atlas of Native Americans,* plus numerous articles. He was an editor of *Astronomy* magazine for several years.

CONTENTS

We live in an enormously large place – the Universe. It's just in the last fifty-five years or so that we've found out how large it probably is. It's only natural that we would want to understand the place in which we live, so scientists have developed instruments – such as radio telescopes, satellites, probes, and many more – that have told us far more about the Universe than could possibly be imagined.

We have seen planets up close. We have learned about quasars and pulsars, black holes, and supernovas. We have gathered amazing data about how the Universe may have come into being and how it may end. Nothing could be more astonishing.

But in all the unbelievably vast Universe, there is only one world that we call home, where the drama of life as we know it began. That world is Earth, one small planet circling one middle-sized star in a corner of a single, unremarkable galaxy. Yet, Earth is an incredibly fascinating place, filled with marvels and miracles.

Isaac Asimov

Above: Planets form in the swirling disk of gas and dust surrounding the newborn Sun.

Right: The young Earth sweeps up some of the rocky leftovers of the Solar System's birth.

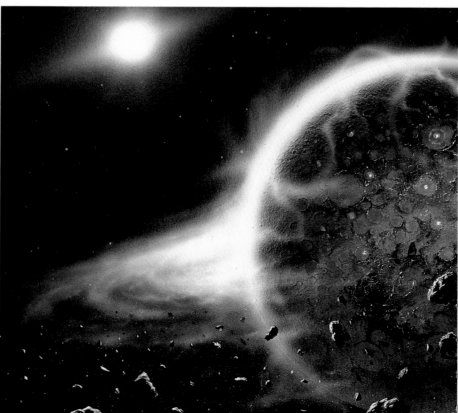

Earth's Beginning

Nearly five billion years ago, there was a vast cloud of dust and gas that was slowly swirling in the sky. Its gravitational pull forced the cloud's elements tighter and tighter together. As the cloud grew smaller, it whirled faster and grew hotter at its center.

Beyond the center of the cloud, the dust and gas built up and formed rocks and boulders. The very center of the cloud became so hot that a star developed – our Sun.

Meanwhile, the rocks and boulders gradually came together with leftover gas to form the planets of our Solar System. One of the planets that formed was our Earth!

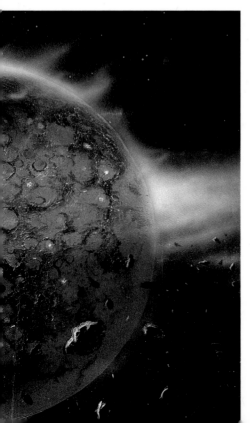

The Composition of Earth

Earth was quite hot as it formed, and the last pieces that joined it left marks on the planet's surface. These marks are called craters.

Water and gases were trapped in the rocks. The water and gases slowly fizzed out to form Earth's atmosphere and vast oceans.

Slowly, the heaviest parts of Earth – metals, such as iron and nickel – settled to the center and melted to form a hot metal core. Around the core, a rocky mantle of solid matter formed. The mantle is hot enough to be slightly soft. The rock in the mantle slowly moves.

Top: A slice of Earth reveals its various layers.

Opposite, bottom: Glowing as it travels through the atmosphere, rocky debris crashes onto the young Earth's hot surface.

Far right: Even today, gases escape from within our planet.

Right: The Moon's craters were caused by collisions with meteorites.

6

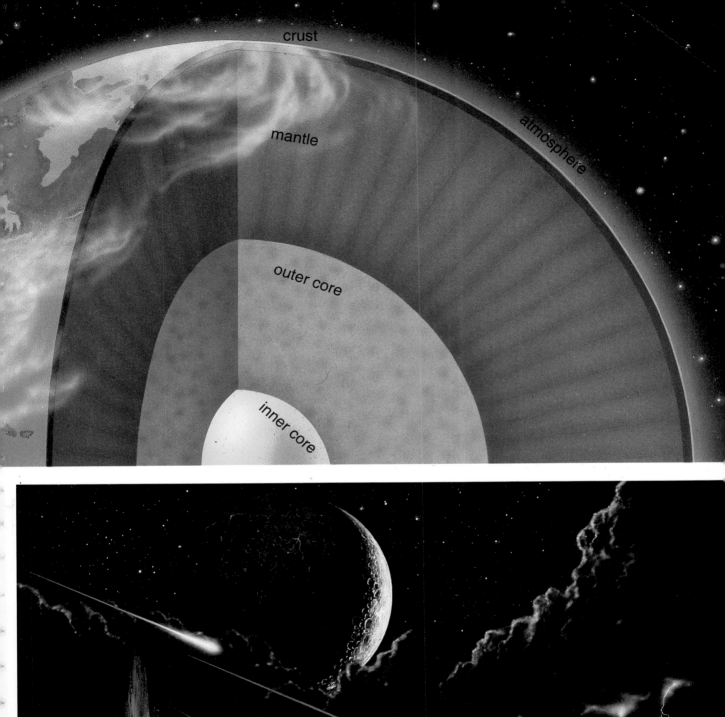

crust

mantle

atmosphere

outer core

inner core

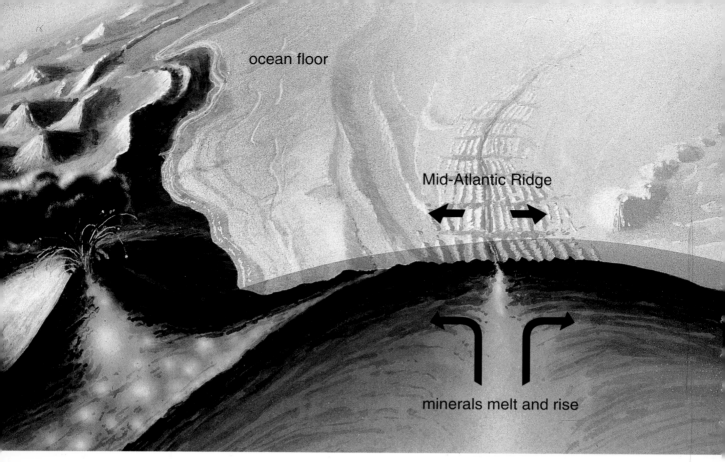

ocean floor

Mid-Atlantic Ridge

minerals melt and rise

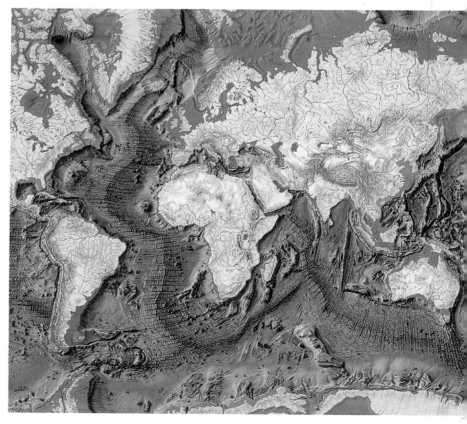

Constantly Changing Earth

Earth's crust is not one solid shell. It is broken into many pieces called plates. These plates move slowly and steadily, constantly changing the surface of Earth.

About 240 million years ago, all of Earth's major landmasses were assembled in a single supercontinent. Scientists call this early continent Pangea. As Earth's wandering plates continued to move, Pangea slowly rifted apart, and the continents we know today began to take shape.

Where the plates pull apart, hot rock comes up from below and forms mountains in the middle of ocean floors. Sometimes the tops of the mountains are visible above the ocean. We call these mountaintops islands – such as the Hawaiian Islands or the Azores.

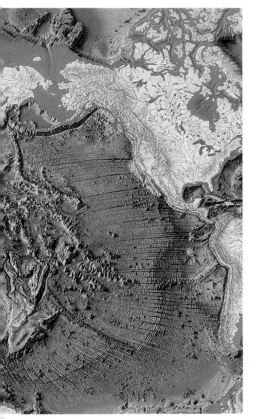

Top: Hot rock from deep within our Earth builds the mountains as the ocean floor spreads apart.

Opposite, bottom: Earth looked quite different millions of years ago. At one time, all the major land areas were joined together in one giant continent called Pangea.

Left: Earth's largest mountain range lies under the water. The Mid-Atlantic Ridge divides the Atlantic Ocean down the middle. This range is 10,000 miles (16,000 kilometers) in length.

! Our Earth – what a waterful world!

Earth's oceans are much larger than Earth's continents. Europe, Asia, and Africa have a combined area of 33 million square miles (85 million sq. km). But the Pacific Ocean alone is 64 million square miles (165 million sq. km). If you count the other oceans, seas, gulfs, and bays, about 71 percent of Earth's surface is covered with water!

Mountains and Earthquakes

Just as the plates are pulling apart in some places, they are forced to come together in other places. This collision of plates can cause the crust to crumple.

Tens of millions of years ago, India "bumped" into Asia, and the crumpling of the crust created the Himalaya Mountains. The Rocky Mountains in North America were created by the collision of the Pacific and North American plates.

Sometimes, the plates rub past one another. But when this happens, the plates don't slide smoothly. They jerk along, under great tension. We feel this as an earthquake. The boundaries of the sliding plates are marked by faults, or cracks, across Earth's surface.

❓ *Mt. Everest – just a sinking sensation?*

Earth's oceans are deeper than its mountains are high! The highest mountain on Earth is Mt. Everest. Its peak is 29,028 feet (about 5.5 miles or 8.9 km) above sea level. But at a place in the Pacific Ocean called the Challenger Deep, the ocean floor is 36,161 feet (about 6.8 miles or 11 km) below sea level. If Mt. Everest could be placed into the Challenger Deep, the entire mountain would disappear with plenty of room to spare!

Top: The San Andreas Fault in California. Pressure builds as plates try to grind past each other. When the rocks give way, an earthquake occurs.

Bottom: Mt. Everest, the highest mountain on Earth, rises in the eastern Himalayas between Nepal and Tibet.

Opposite: Earthquakes can reshape the land and topple buildings, such as these in Los Angeles in 1994 *(top)* and San Francisco in 1989 *(bottom)*.

10

A Violent Upheaval

Where plates meet, one plate slides under the other. As the plate sinks, its rock is heated to the melting point. This melted rock makes its way upward and produces volcanoes.

In Hawaii, there is an active volcano, called Kilauea, where melted rock, or lava, sometimes overflows in a river of fire. In the Philippines in 1991, a volcano named Mt. Pinatubo underwent a dramatic eruption that shot a cloud of ash 25 miles (40 km) high. It was the biggest eruption the world had seen since 1912.

Most of the ocean floor beneath the Pacific is one big plate. All around its edge, there are volcanoes and earthquakes. Because of all this activity, the edge is known as the Ring of Fire.

Violent activities, such as earthquakes and volcanic eruptions, are Earth's way of adjusting to changing pressures at and below its surface. But these events can harm people and other living things and damage homes and habitat.

! *The island that exploded*

The greatest volcanic eruption in modern times took place in 1883 on a little Indonesian island called Krakatau. When that island – which was actually a volcano – exploded, it created a huge wave of water that washed over nearby shores and destroyed 163 villages. Over 36,000 people died. The explosion was so loud that it could be heard 3,000 miles (4,800 km) away. Rocks were hurled 34 miles (55 km) into the air. Luckily, volcanoes rarely explode.

Opposite: On June 12, 1991, Mt. Pinatubo began its first major eruption in over six hundred years. The volcano exploded a few days later.

Left: The volcano Parícutin in Mexico started as a smoking crack in a cornfield. Within eight months, it destroyed two villages and grew to over 1,500 feet (457 m) high.

Earth's Active Atmosphere

Earth is surrounded by a vast amount of air. At first, this atmosphere was made up of nitrogen and carbon dioxide. But as simple forms of life developed, they changed the carbon dioxide to oxygen. This made it possible for people and animals to breathe. In turn, when people and animals exhale, or breathe out, they return carbon dioxide to the air.

The atmosphere is unevenly heated by the Sun. Warm air rises and cold air sinks. This sets up a movement that creates the winds. When ocean water evaporates, it cools and is changed into clouds in the upper air. The clouds are made of water droplets. Eventually, the water returns to Earth in the form of rain. Sometimes, the combination of rain and wind can result in violent storms, such as hurricanes and tornadoes.

Opposite – top/bottom, left: Thunderstorms bring strong winds and lightning – even hurricanes and tornadoes.

Opposite – bottom, right: Plants use the gases people and animals exhale to make their food – and to make the oxygen people and animals need to breathe.

Below: Earth's atmosphere wasn't always as welcoming to living things as it is in present times.

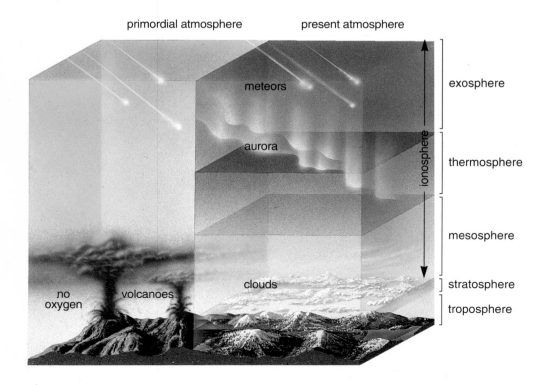

primordial atmosphere | present atmosphere

meteors — exosphere

aurora — thermosphere

ionosphere

mesosphere

clouds — stratosphere

troposphere

no oxygen | volcanoes

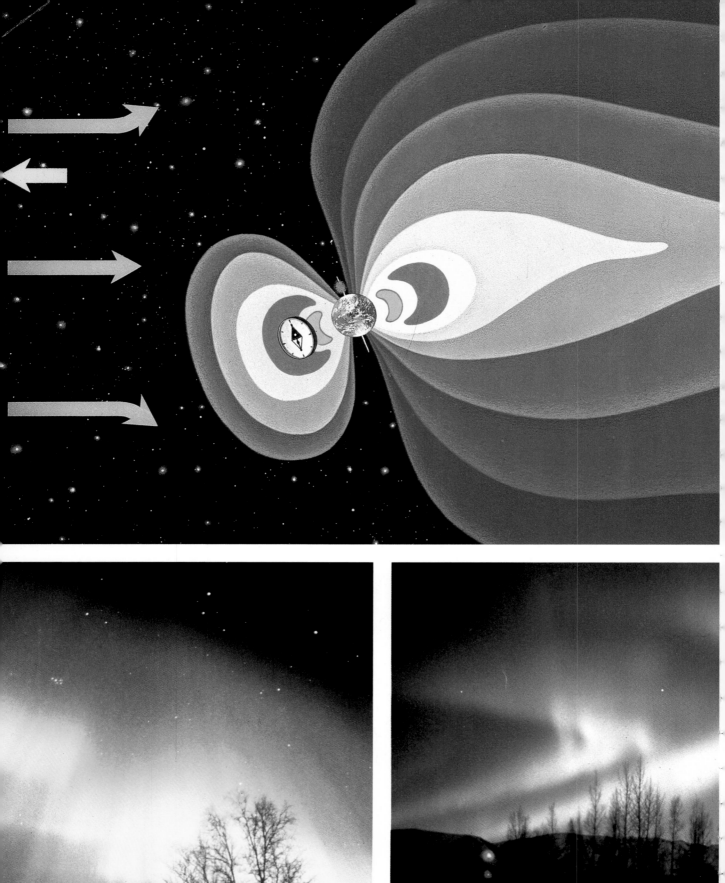

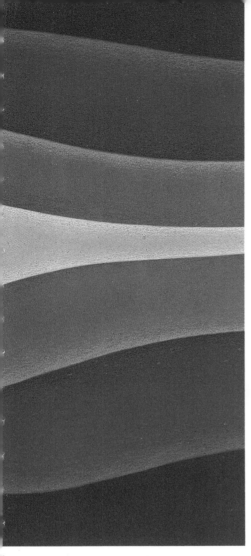

Earth's Magnetic Attraction

As Earth turns, the melted iron within its central core swirls. The swirling iron sets up a magnetic field that surrounds Earth. This makes Earth a gigantic magnet! This magnetism allows compasses to work. Compass needles continually point toward Earth's magnetic poles.

The Sun is always giving off particles that have electric charges. This is called the solar wind. Solar wind could harm Earth, but it becomes trapped in Earth's magnetic field before it can reach us. At Earth's polar regions, however, some of the particles do reach our atmosphere. This makes the atmosphere glow in a spectacular sight called the aurora.

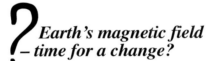

Earth's magnetic field – time for a change?

Earth's magnetic field sometimes weakens, reverses itself, and then grows stronger. If this happened today, a compass that was pointing north would begin to point south. Scientists know that Earth has had many magnetic reversals, although the last one happened 730,000 years ago. No one knows how or why they occur. But Earth's magnetic field has been getting weaker since 1835. If this continues, it will have no strength at all in about 1,700 years. Perhaps there's a magnetic reversal coming up!

Top: Particles from the distant Sun *(unseen, at left)* pull and stretch Earth's magnetic field. Most of the particles flow around the magnetic field, but some of them become trapped inside it. These particles usually enter the atmosphere over Earth's poles.

Bottom (both photos): When solar particles collide with gases in Earth's atmosphere, the gas atoms give off light. This phenomenon is called an aurora. Auroras can be as colorful as a rainbow, but they are usually green or blue-green.

Understanding Our World through Others

Like Earth, Mars has polar ice caps, and each day is about twenty-four hours long. But Mars is much colder than Earth. Venus has a thicker cloud layer and atmosphere than Earth. The Great Red Spot on Jupiter is really a giant storm – like a hurricane that seems to go on forever. One of Jupiter's satellites, Io, has volcanic eruptions.

Our Moon has no air or water and has changed very little over time. By studying the Moon closely, scientists can discover what the Solar System was like in its early days.

What we learn about other worlds can help us understand our own!

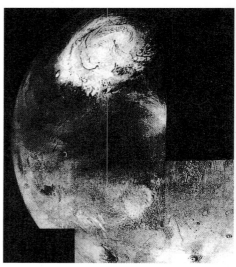

Opposite, top: Astronauts have been able to watch Earth rise over the Moon's surface.

Opposite, bottom: The plume of an erupting volcano rises over Io, a moon of Jupiter.

Top: Like Earth, Mars has ice caps at its northern and southern poles.

Far right: The Great Red Spot, a storm many times larger than Earth, has been seen on Jupiter since the invention of the telescope in 1608.

Right: Thick clouds mask the surface of Venus.

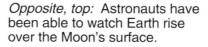

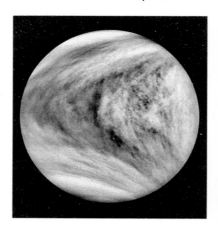

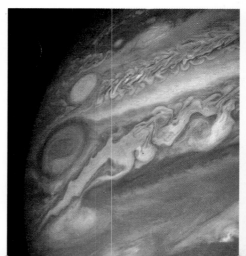

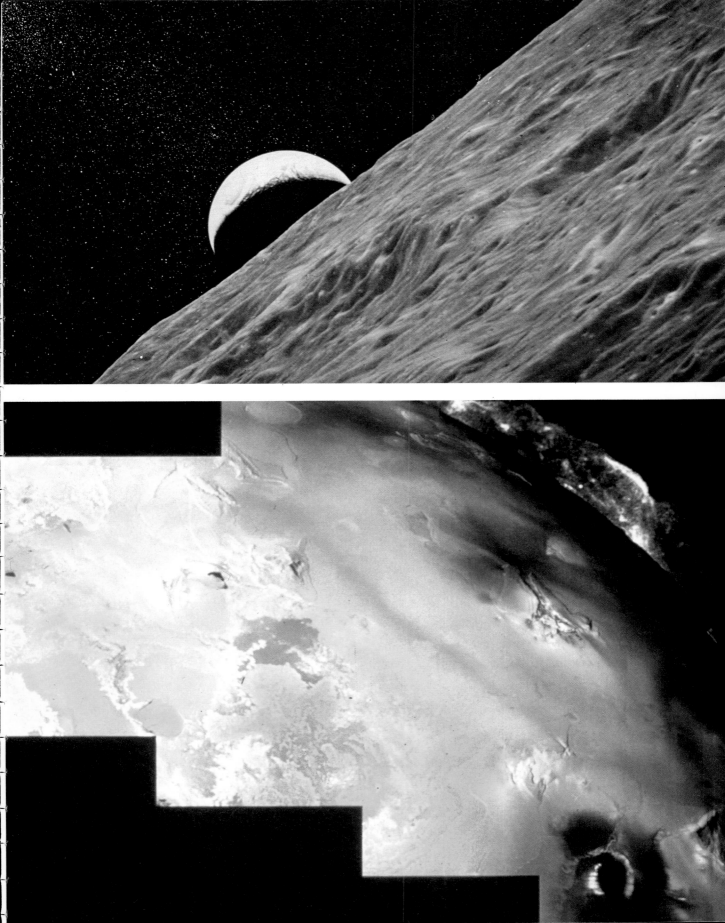

Earth – A Very Special World

Although other planets can help us learn about Earth, our special planet is still quite different from any of the other planets.

Other planets are either too small to hold an atmosphere, or are too hot or too cold for water to stay liquid. Earth has an ocean of water that is needed for life, as we know it, to develop. Earth is just the right size and temperature for life to flourish.

There might be other worlds like Earth circling the stars, but we don't yet know anything about them!

? Deep freeze or hothouse?

Just ten thousand years ago, enormous sheets of ice covered Canada, Scandinavia, and the northern parts of Siberia and the United States. Many scientists think that ice ages come and go because very small changes in Earth's orbit around the Sun cause our planet to cool over thousands of years. On the other hand, many scientists are concerned that human activities will warm the planet over the next few decades. Both theories may be right – depending on how far into the future you look!

Opposite, top: Our awe-inspiring planet Earth.

Top and center: Humans share the planet with a great variety of other life-forms, such as the lemon butterfly fish of Hawaii.

Bottom: Mars, the fourth planet from the Sun, is too cold to sustain life as we know it. Venus, the second planet from the Sun, is too hot. Earth, in between, has just the right conditions for life.

Our Fragile Planet

In future times, Earth might not have ideal conditions for life. Humans do not always treat the planet Earth gently, and our population is ever-increasing. Right now, there are about 5.8 billion of us. We need space and materials, so we cut down Earth's forests, which drives other forms of life into extinction. We pollute the atmosphere and ocean, so the air and water can be dangerous to living things. Through our carelessness, we have thinned the ozone layer, a part of our atmosphere that shields harmful radiation from Earth. Then, too, we have developed nuclear bombs that could potentially make Earth's surface radioactive – and life impossible. We must try to take better care of our precious world!

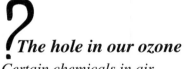

The hole in our ozone

Certain chemicals in air conditioners, spray cans, and other products contain chlorine that damages Earth's ozone layer. Ozone, a form of oxygen, is concentrated about 13.5 miles (22 km) above Earth. Even there, it exists only in small amounts. Ozone shields Earth from the Sun's most harmful ultraviolet light.

Studies have shown that the ozone over Antarctica becomes very thin each spring. Scientists named this area the "ozone hole." Much smaller losses of ozone have occurred in other parts of the world, too. If we reduce our use of ozone-destroying chemicals, it is possible that ozone damage can be eliminated one day.

Opposite, top: The ozone hole over Antarctica has gotten bigger in recent years. As the amount of damaging chlorine in the atmosphere increases, the amount of protective ozone decreases. *Opposite, bottom, left:* Air pollution from smokestacks.

Opposite, bottom, right (two images): The world's rain forests are shrinking. The trees are cut down so the land may be used by certain people to make profits.

Wildlife suffers greatly due to the careless actions of humans. *Top:* This gull died as a result of becoming trapped in a plastic beverage ring.

Bottom: A dolphin lost its life after accidentally becoming entangled in a fishing net.

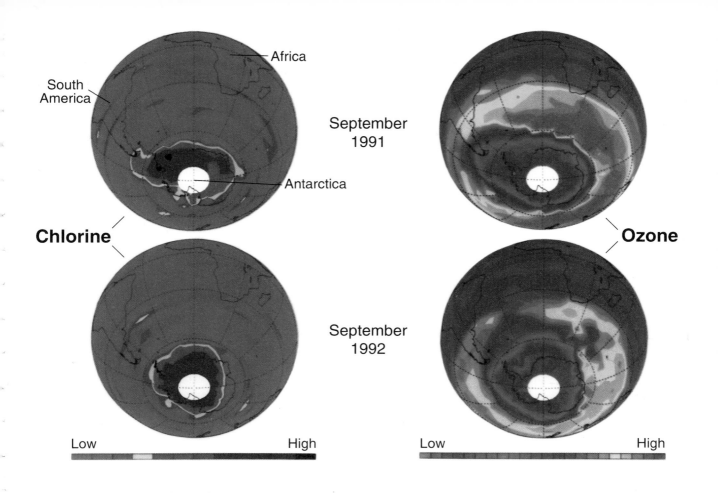

South
America

Africa

Antarctica

September
1991

September
1992

Chlorine

Ozone

Low | High

Low | High

The Worlds Beyond

Konstantin Tsiolkovsky, a Russian scientist and rocket pioneer, said, "Earth is humanity's cradle, but you can't stay in the cradle forever."

In 1969, a human stepped on the Moon for the first time in history. So far, a total of twelve people have walked on the Moon. Scientists are making plans for humans to visit Mars some day. At some point in the near future, there will be permanent space stations in outer space, where people will live and work. One day, there may be entire cities in space, where thousands of people will make their homes.

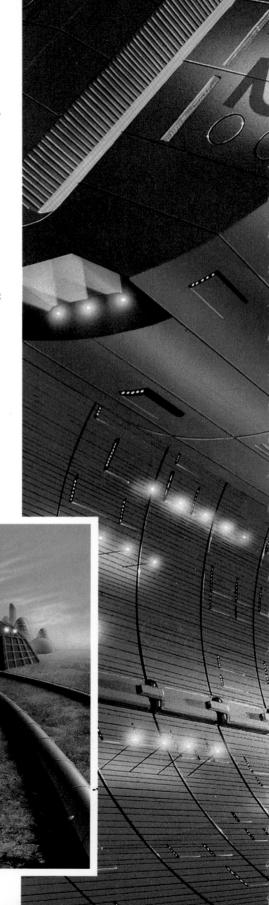

Opposite: We are just beginning to explore the possibilities of permanent human habitation in space.

Right: One day, we may have the technology to make pollution from motorized vehicles and industries a thing of the past.

Terraforming Other Worlds

People may one day live in domed cities on the Moon and Mars. Or we may live underneath the ground on these new worlds. It might even be possible to bring water and oxygen to Mars and make the conditions there similar to Earth's. We might be able to take some of the carbon dioxide away from Venus and add oxygen. That would cool Venus, which is now too hot for life as we know it.

Terraforming other planets, or making them like Earth, is something that we will be able to do in the future. Then, too, the day will come when we can visit the stars. We might discover planets so similar to Earth, they will not need terraforming!

But for now, Earth's future is our future. Let's take good care of our Earth!

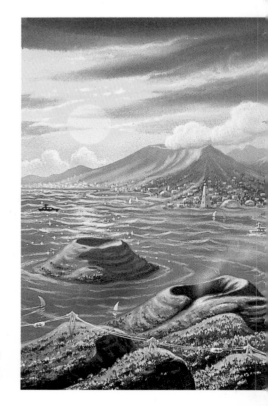

Opposite: It's hard to imagine a time when your school might be on a rocket ship, but it could happen!

Right: As we travel to other worlds, we might try to change their climates to suit human life. Perhaps the Sun will one day peek through the thick clouds of Venus to shine on a beach filled with vacationers.

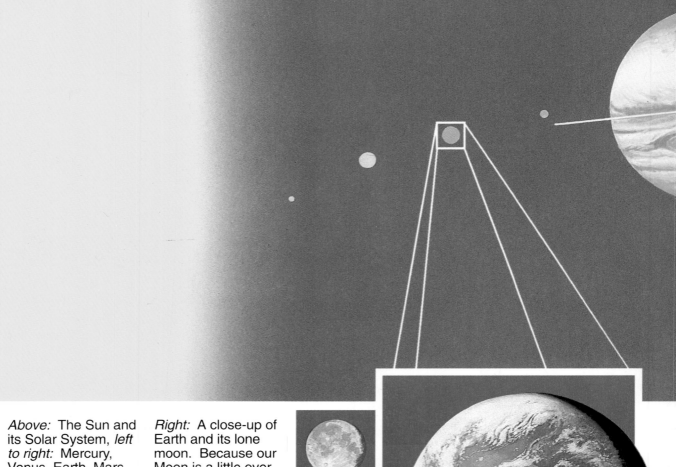

Above: The Sun and its Solar System, *left to right:* Mercury, Venus, Earth, Mars, Jupiter, Saturn, Uranus, Neptune, and Pluto.

Right: A close-up of Earth and its lone moon. Because our Moon is a little over one-fourth as wide as Earth, the two could be thought of as a double planet.

Earth's Moon

Diameter	Distance from Earth's Center	Percentage of Earth's Diameter
2,160 miles (3,475 km)	242,930 miles (390,940 km)	27.25%

Compared to What We Think Is Big on Earth, Earth Is . . .

- **so wide** that if you could drill a giant hole through it and fill the hole with the world's tallest building, you could stuff 28,783 Sears Towers into the hole and still not have anything sticking out. The Sears Tower in Chicago, Illinois, is the world's tallest building at 1,454 feet (443.18 meters).
- **so big** around that if you could drive around the world at 55 miles (88.5 km) an hour without stopping, it would take you about 453 hours before you returned from where you started. That's almost nineteen days of nonstop driving!

But Earth Is Also…

- **so tiny** compared to the Sun that you could stuff more than a million Earths in the space the Sun takes up!
- **so far away from Mars** that it would take you about a year to get there and another year to come back!
- **our little planet.** As any astronomer or astronaut can tell you, our little planet takes up just a speck in space. But that little speck is where we live – and the place from which we can study the rest of our vast Universe.

Fact File: Our Special Home – Earth

Earth is the fifth largest known planet in our Solar System, and the third closest to the Sun. It is the largest of the inner planets – just over 7,926 miles (12,756 km) wide. This means that our planet is about 5 percent bigger than Venus, almost twice the diameter of Mars, and more than 2.5 times the diameter of Mercury.

Earth is also the heaviest inner planet of our Solar System. It weighs about 6.59 sextillion tons. It is about 23 percent heavier than Venus, 9.5 times heavier than Mars, and more than 18 times the mass of Mercury.

But Earth is still only a speck when compared with even an average star, like our Sun. The Sun is more than 108 times the diameter of Earth. And the Sun is almost 333,000 times as heavy!

Earth may not be that big, but it is very special. It is the place that humans and other living things call home. Humans must learn to live in harmony with all beings, not only on Earth but wherever we travel in the Universe.

More Books about Earth

All about Deserts. Sanders (Troll)
Animals of the Tropical Forests. Johnson (Franklin Watts)
Arctic and Antarctic Regions. Sabin (Troll)
Earth Afire! Volcanoes and Their Activity. Fodor (Morrow)
Exploring Our World (series). Jennings (Marshall Cavendish)
Our Planetary System. Asimov (Gareth Stevens)
Trees Alive. Riedman (Lothrop, Lee and Shepard)

Video

Our Solar System. (Gareth Stevens)

Places to Visit

To study the rest of the Universe from our Earthly home, visit these museums and centers where you can find a variety of space exhibits.

The Space and Rocket Center
  and Space Camp
One Tranquility Base
Huntsville, AL 35807

National Air and Space Museum
Smithsonian Institution
Seventh and Independence Avenue SW
Washington, D.C. 20560

Anglo-Australian Observatory
Private Bag
Coonarbariban 2357 Australia

Astrocentre
Royal Ontario Museum
100 Queen's Park
Toronto, Ontario M5S 2C6

San Diego Aero-Space Museum
2001 Pan American Plaza
Balboa Park
San Diego, CA 92101

Seneca College Planetarium
1750 Finch Avenue East
North York, Ontario M2J 2X5

Places to Write

Here are some places you can write for more information about studying our Universe from Earth. Be sure to state what kind of information you would like. Include your full name and address so they can write back to you.

Sydney Observatory
P. O. Box K346
Haymarket 2000 Australia

NASA Lewis Research Center
Educational Services Office
21000 Brookpark Road
Cleveland, OH 44135

National Space Society
922 Pennsylvania Avenue SE
Washington, D.C. 20003

Canadian Space Agency
Communications Department
6767 Route de L'Aeroport
Saint Hubert, Quebec J3Y 8Y9

Glossary

atmosphere: the gases that surround a planet, star, or moon.

aurora: light at the North and South poles of Earth caused by the collision of solar wind with Earth's outer atmosphere.

billion: the number represented by 1 followed by nine zeroes – 1,000,000,000. In some countries, this number is called "a thousand million." In these countries, one billion would then be represented by 1 followed by twelve zeroes – 1,000,000,000,000 – a million million.

carbon dioxide: early in the history of our planet, one of the main gases, along with nitrogen, that made up Earth's atmosphere. When humans and animals breathe out, they exhale carbon dioxide.

continents: large land bodies surrounded by water on Earth's surface.

core: the central part. The core of Earth is believed to consist mainly of iron and nickel.

craters: holes or pits on planets and moons created by the impact of meteorites or volcanic explosions.

crust: the outermost solid layer, including the surface area.

diameter: the distance across or the width of something.

evaporate: to change from a liquid into a vapor or a gas.

extinction: the dying out of a life-form. Many plants and animals are in danger of extinction.

fault: a break in Earth's crust often found where plates come together.

ice ages: periods in the history of Earth that saw the movement of great ice glaciers across parts of the land surface of the planet.

magnetic field: a field around Earth caused by the planet's rotation, which makes the melted iron in Earth's core swirl. As a result, Earth behaves like a huge magnet.

mantle: the hot, rocky matter that surrounds Earth's core.

mass: a quantity, or amount, of matter.

oxygen: the gas in Earth's atmosphere that makes human and animal life possible.

ozone layer: that part of our atmosphere that shields us from the Sun's dangerous ultraviolet rays.

Pangea: the giant single continent that made up the land surface of Earth hundreds of millions of years ago.

plates: sections of Earth's crust created by the movement of rock in Earth's mantle.

solar wind: tiny particles that travel from the Sun's surface at a speed of about 250 miles (402 km) a second.

terraforming: making another world like Earth by providing it with substances that are, as far as we know, special to Earth, such as oxygen and water.

Index

Born in 1920, Isaac Asimov came to the United States as a young boy from his native Russia. As a young man, he was a student of biochemistry. In time, he became one of the most productive writers the world has ever known. His books cover a spectrum of topics, including science, history, language theory, fantasy, and science fiction. His brilliant imagination gained him the respect and admiration of adults and children alike. Sadly, Isaac Asimov died shortly after the publication of the first edition of *Isaac Asimov's Library of the Universe*.

The publishers wish to thank the following for permission to reproduce copyright material: front cover, NASA; 4-5 (both), © John Foster 1988; 6 (left), Lick Observatory; 6 (right), © William Hartmann; 6-7, © Lynette Cook 1988; 7, © John Foster 1988; 8, © Julian Baum 1988; 8-9 (upper), © Garret Moore 1988; 8-9 (lower), © Hachette Guides; 10 (upper), R. E. Wallace/USGS; 10 (lower), © 1995 Dave Bartruff; 11 (both), NOAA; 12, K. Jackson, U.S. Air Force; 13, K. Segerstrum/USGS; 14, © Garret Moore 1988; 15 (upper and lower left), National Severe Storms Laboratory; 15 (lower right), © Mark Maxwell 1988; 16, © Forrest Baldwin; 16-17 (upper), © Lynette Cook 1988; 16-17 (lower), © Forrest Baldwin; 18 (all), 18-19, NASA; 19, Jet Propulsion Laboratory; 20, NASA; 20-21 (upper), © Chappell Studio; 20-21 (center), © Brian Parker/Tom Stack and Associates; 20-21 (lower), © Tom Miller; 22 (upper), U.S. Fish and Wildlife Service Photo by P. Martinkovic; 22 (lower), © Dave Falzetti/Greenpeace; 23 (upper), NASA; 23 (lower left), © Gary Milburn/Tom Stack and Associates; 23 (center and lower right), © Rain Forest Action Network; 24, 24-25, © Doug McLeod 1988; 26-27, © David A. Hardy 1988; 27, © Pat Rawlings; 28-29 (all), © Sally Bensusen 1988.